Sad Girl Sitting
on a Running Board

# Sad Girl Sitting on a Running Board

*Poems by* Michael McFee

GNOMON PRESS

FIRST EDITION

This project is supported
by a grant from the National
Endowment for the Arts, a Federal
Agency.

Copyright (c) 1991 by Michael McFee

LCC NUMBER 91-72899

ISBN 0-917788-49-4

*Published by* Gnomon Press,
P.O. Box 475, Frankfort,
Kentucky 40602–0475

*Cover drawing by Leah Palmer Preiss*

*To the memory of my father*
WILLIAM HOWARD MCFEE

CONTENTS

I.

FUNERAL HOME     3
BURIAL EVE     5
FUNERAL     6
INVENTORY     7

II.

SAD GIRL SITTING ON A RUNNING BOARD     13
TINTED PICTURES     14
LOOK     15
AWFUL     16
MY MOTHER AND CLARK GABLE
    ON THE WORLD'S MOST FAMOUS BEACH     17
DOUBLED     18

III.

NEWLYWEDS     23
VENUS AND MARS     24
MARRIED COUPLES ON VACATION     25
SHOWER     26
YOUNG FAMILY ON VACATION     27
THERE'S NOTHING FINER THAN A BOY!     28
VANISHING ACT     30

## IV.

POCKET WATCH 35
WILDER BRAIN COLLECTION,
    CORNELL UNIVERSITY 38
SECRETS 42
LAST BIRTHDAY 46


## V.

GRACE 51

ACKNOWLEDGMENTS

Thanks to these magazines, their editors and readers, for first publishing these poems:

*Poetry:* "Sad Girl Sitting on a Running Board"
*Hudson Review:* "Wilder Brain Collection, Cornell University"
*Southern Review:* "Look"
*Shenandoah:* "There's Nothing Finer Than a Boy!"
*New Virginia Review:* "Newlyweds," "Shower," "Secrets"
*Southern Humanities Review:* "Venus and Mars"
*Potato Eyes:* "Vanishing Act"
*Bloodroot to Summit:* "Tinted Pictures"
*Turning Dances:* "Young Family on Vacation"
*Wolfpen Branch:* "Funeral Home," "Burial Eve," "Funeral," "Inventory"
*Iris:* "Married Couples on Vacation"

Special thanks to Mickey Pruett, who has provided inspiration and information for so many years.

# I

# FUNERAL HOME

*Whose mother is this? Whose wife?*
*Whose daughter, long gone?*

This is the mouth of a fifth-grade teacher,
stern yet prim, lips
taut with permanent displeasure, face
haunted by the shadow of a frown.

*It was the late futile kiss of oxygen*
*that did this.*

This is a mannequin's coiffure,
too deliberately clipped, laid to rest
strand by turgid strand.
It does sort of resemble hair—from a distance,
if you squint.

*It was a fully certified stranger*
*that did this to her.*

Whose manicured hands are these,
so meekly folded, heaped
in such a pious gravelike mound over the heart?

*They should be throttling a cup of coffee,*
*squeezing its healing heat.*

And whose flimsy glasses,
so precisely posed
over eyes whose lids have been basted shut?

*Those were the first blue worlds
I ever knew.*

This is a poor impersonation
but they did their best. We'll switch off the light
as we leave, and wait for my real mother
to slip from the coffin's pocket,
her stocking-feet crackling across the carpet . . .

*It's not like her, dad says in the hall.
Not like her at all.*

## BURIAL EVE

All night dad circulates the house
like a deep-sea fish inspecting a wreck.

He shuffles and pulses his flashlight
off the furniture, a nervous thief.

Nothing changes, but everything's changed.
He paces the sunken darkness and blinks.

He checks on me in my wagon-train bed
as if I were six. He touches the covers

and sighs. I pretend to stir in my sleep,
again. He resumes his ghostly cruise.

The pressure per inch on the anglerfish
waiting for prey on the ocean floor

must be enormous, water darker than oil.
Morning is miles above our breathing.

## FUNERAL

I remember the ride to the grave, in a blue limousine.
The funeral home director talked about his college days.
We filed through the predicted rain into a low green tent.
The coffin on its hydraulic lift took up most of the space.
It seemed to grow bigger and colder as the preacher went on.
The preacher didn't know my mother, but he tried to save us.
My sister in her new dress and sandals shivered to my left.
My father in his dark suit and wingtips shivered to my right.
I shivered with them and for us all, in that February cold.
I accidentally stamped my foot, and the preacher shut up.
There were pallbearers, friends, a quick shaking of hands.
We walked to the limousine under vast black umbrellas.
We sat on the overstuffed seats and glided back home.

# INVENTORY

### 1.

Under her bed: a dust-cloud
and this cuff. She'd stubbornly lace it up
by herself, with her teeth and one free hand,
whenever the arthritis got really bad.

Its soft leather is stained
as an old ballglove, its felt lining
embossed like a death-mask of her wrist.

### 2.

On the bedside table: her "scratch pad,"
a bibliography of dog-eared Romance,
those dim gothic nightcaps
she'd sip for a few minutes before sleep

only to wake at three a.m.
with another crippling crick in her neck,
stuck on the same page as the night before.

Their titles were such a blur
of mist and mystery,
she always carried this list to the branch library.

3.

On the closet shelves: an avalanche
of papers, a sentimental archive
of documents from her devoted children—

crayon portraits of our family
planted like smiling shrubs in the yard,

a construction-paper Coat of Many Colors
that opens to the moral GOD IS GOOD
on its lining, in mom's own hand,

a rebus that looks like a ransom note
but sounds out YOU ARE THE BEST
  MOTHER IN THE WORLD.

And a box of seashells we casually collected
almost three decades ago,
bags of sand dollars devalued to sand.

4.

Cash at the back of her dresser drawer.
Cash tucked in pockets like a folded handkerchief.
Cash in a strongbox.
Cash in a shoe box.
Cash rubber banded in used envelopes.

Cash the banks would never again have a chance to lose.

5.

And pictures, pictures, pictures
chinked everywhere around the house,

over half a century of snapshots
stuffed into drugstore bags

and albums, swollen folios
regathering the scattered family

into a kind of story, a fitful order.
I ease some pictures from the seats

my mother found time to assign them.
Their crisp corner mounts remain

pasted to the page, black arrows
framing bricked-up windows, chevrons

sprinkled from a soldier's shoulder
as he salutes a grave, a hiatus

in this text of light—these incidental
stills that still tell a life.

· II ·

# SAD GIRL SITTING ON A RUNNING BOARD

She thinks we'll notice her feet first,
laced into tire-colored brogans,
or the way her hand-me-down stockings
stop in a homely doughnut just below the knee,
or how cheap her crumpled sackdress looks
despite piping at collar and cuff.

But it's the painful focus of her face
that stops us, trapped in its pageboy haircut
like chain mail, the gravity already
eroding her eyes and mouth and shoulders,
the world-weariness of those arms
folded in a half-hearted cross on her chest.

It's that eye-level shadow of a hand
pressed into the dusty car door beside her
like fate waiting in an x-ray film,
rising to the breath-warmed surface of a dream
as if to say *Halt, beware, stay back,*
leaving its oily ghost of touch.

# TINTED PICTURES

Someone has swabbed in a rosy horizon,
a too-blue sky. There stand my sober
mother and her big sister, by the Pigeon
River, its skin a cheap hopeful mirror

of the sky. The backdrop trees, though
leafless, are a queasy rash of green,
like the grass underfoot in God's studio,
the deep fall mountains of nineteen,

what, twenty-seven? The girls pose
unretouched, awkward as brothers whose
mother has caught them in stolen clothes—
smocks, stockings, high-laced shoes,

worn britches hidden behind their backs.
The river drawls their secret to the bridge,
also untinted, its smooth concrete span
a perfect echo of the distant ridge,

and it sends the hint of its new highway
back through the young one's head, the idea
of riding all alone through a gap one day
to a world too quick for any camera.

But for now she has to wait, content
with this tousle of grass by the river,
with this stiff face, with the curious tint
that some stranger's hand may give her.

## LOOK

How Lois delights in this blur
on her lap!—the unexpected
sister a dozen years younger,

Molly, a quick cheeky girl whose
coming has soaked the venom
from the bite of the Depression.

How Lois loves to balance that
baby on a skinny jutted hip
until her forearm goes to sleep,

to kiss that head's soft spot
thinner now than a dime
under its sweet fire of hair.

How this deadpan little girl
makes them all laugh, even
here in an overgrown graveyard:

Lois, smelling Molly's bonnet;
her mama, hands locked in prayer
for that windfall baby; her daddy,

squinting at them from the far side
of the lens, calling *Look! look!*,
flapping a free hand over his head

as the camera takes a slice of light
from the women and, beyond them,
a headstone that seems to read DADDY.

# AWFUL

"Isn't this AWFUL?" my mother has scrawled
across the bottom of this candid snapshot.
She and her roommate Martha march in step
down a downtown sidewalk, back to work.
They have just finished business college,
it's their first job, their first apartment.
Martha wears solid black, her hat, her shoes,
the coat she hides her weary hands inside.
Lois wears saddle oxfords and bobby socks,
a flared plaid coat with wide white lapels,
no hat. She looks like she's just snapped
her long fingers, to kick off the downbeat
of a popular tune, or to remind herself
of something she needs to buy on lunch break,
something she keeps forgetting. Her father
has been dead a year or so, a suicide,
everyone says. He drank some metal cleaner
in his shop one foggy fall night. He liked
to drink. She wonders if it wasn't just
a mistake, if daddy hadn't meant to lift
the hidden moonshine from an upper shelf
and got the unmarked acid instead. She tries
not to think how that last shocking drink
must have felt going down, the awful draft
scalding him alive, from the inside out . . .

She snaps her fingers to forget. Somebody
on the corner snaps this picture. The words
DAIRY PRODUCTS and SODA snap on a marquee
over her head as she walks back to work.
There are thirsty people all around her.

# MY MOTHER AND CLARK GABLE ON THE WORLD'S MOST FAMOUS BEACH

The racy Atlantic pounds behind them
as it has been paid to, the sun flatters
the back of her knee, He is everything
an idol should be—tall, slick, ironic,

and fake. Behind his broad right shoulder
a strut protrudes like a clipped wing,
illogical details darken his charm,
his body tilts stiffly into my mother,

who doesn't seem to notice. She drapes
a slim arm around his neck, her fingertips
tease his collar-hairs, her other hand
straightens the crisp Windsor of his tie,

her body casts its indelible shadow
of desire his entire cardboard length.
One windblown hair tickles his mustache.
Clark smiles, she smiles, the famous

Daytona sun cackles overhead, the pier
in the background chuckles to itself
as it stabs Gable in his false back
like a jealous ex-lover, hers or his.

## DOUBLED

1.

Once I found our family treed
on the endpapers of a slipcased book
hidden under granny's rotten Bible,
*America's Constitutional Heritage.*
My mother's name was yoked to some man
I'd never heard of. I thrust the book
at her in the kitchen and demanded,
"Who *is* this?"—such a little lawyer,
presenting his surprise evidence!

"Oh, that was my first husband,"
she said, and kept on mashing potatoes.

2.

I felt strangely distanced from myself,
the bodies I had become: one the real *me*
leaning against the familiar fridge,

the other the boy I might have been
if this stranger had become my father,
the Doppelgänger always haunting me.

3.

*I am shivering behind a column,
watching someone pace a perfect radius
to the center of the rotunda.*

*The sky's cold eye peers down
as he turns toward me, and suddenly
I realize what's so dangerously wrong:*

*he is me, and if our eyes connect
and he speaks the secret already melting
on his tongue, I will die.*

But I don't. I wake up, every time.

4.

And now I finally see him, that man
my mother buried in a book, a single photo
plastered to this loose album page.

He's not much older than I was
when I accidentally discovered his name,
a lanky kid with delicate features.

He stands on an office stoop wondering
which *him* my mother will see: the boy
he feels like, with fine vain hair
swooping across a smooth forehead,

or the man everybody keeps telling him
he must be, trapped inside the dark ghost
of this heavy double-breasted coat
and these weathered shoes and gloves,

his hat jammed back like a black halo.

## NEWLYWEDS

There's nothing original about them—
another couple married in the corner parlor
and posed afterwards in the justice's side yard
wearing the same cut of suit and carnation
as dozens of others that postwar October.

There's not a clue to the future or past
in the carpet of shadow unrolling from them,
the flower-girl leaves crushed underfoot.

There's only the usual background traffic
and the paid lady photographer who snaps
"OK, kids, look married" then this picture

and them, her arm hooking his, that link
the first in another chain of family,
suffering this staged exchange of smiles
like ambassadors from rival nations
whose hearts have privately burst into bloom.

## VENUS AND MARS

The young gods pose with their honeymoon coupé,
the love they worked all afternoon to erase
from the car still glowing in their faces.

My mother perches on the back fender, her feet
lightly buffing the bumper where the kite-
tail of K-rations heckled them down the street.

My father balances on the ornate proscenium
around the license plate, polishing the chrome
on the tailpipe's fancy flange with his thumb.

There's a fine crackling calm about them. See
how she can't keep her bright nails from dancing,
how even his second hand won't stop pulsing?

## MARRIED COUPLES ON VACATION

My mother oils my father's thighs
but he is sleepy, he has just waxed
his black Buick with the whalebone grill
parked right beside them on the beach.
She watches him nap in the hubcap.

My mother takes my father's picture
on the pier, he and his pal from work
have been deep-sea fishing all afternoon.
They hoist their modest catch for her
to take back to the cottage and clean.

My mother poses her new best friend
on the boardwalk, but she looks worried
and the rail has rusted and the bench
is peeling and that row of dark cars
idles near the horizon like a funeral.

My mother makes snapshots of dolphins,
of hotels and palms and peacocks,
of an empty beach scabbed with seaweed.
"It's not as bad," she writes on the back,
"as this might lead you to believe."

Someone takes matching photographs
of my parents beside a cypress lagoon.
My dad looks away. My mom looks back
as, behind her, a dozen flamingos
all bury their heads in the black water.

## SHOWER

My mother laughs so hard that she goes blind
in this picture, her eyes are soldered shut
by tiny tears. Somebody is making
a funny toast and her friends are smiling
toward the camera with their eyes open,
clutching wrapped boxes, but my mother is

blind, she just can't seem to open her eyes
or stop these loud sobs of laughter that come
from another body. The opened gifts
wait on the desk for her to take them home,
the ladies wait to pass her more presents
so they can play another party game,

the baby that is slowly exploding
her waistline waits for her, the meteor
shower inside her eyelids waits for her
to understand its sign, but she can't stop
laughing so loud her boss looks out his door—
though nothing is that funny anymore.

## YOUNG FAMILY ON VACATION

My dad naps face-down on the beach blanket,
his ballcap shielding his neck, his loud shirt
rolled up so he can get a little tan.
                                      Suddenly
my year-old sister toddles into the picture
and perches on the small of his back. How cute,
she looks like a lucky hunter, my dad the prey
ready to be stuffed!
                        My mother is so tickled
she blurs her daughter's face, her new sunsuit
and hat and sandals. The only thing in focus,
the only other thing in sight along this tilted
stretch of beach, is a STEAMED HOT DOG truck,
BEST IN TOWN, anchored beside the empty Atlantic.
An American flag on the antenna occasionally
stirs in its sleep.
                    My father is awake now,
he's just playing dead, soon the young family
will stroll over for cokes and some lunch
and chase the waves. And this same ocean breeze
that once whispered *love* to my mother and *war*
to my father will say *son* to them both
                                      and they
will stop in the shade of an unrented umbrella
watching their daughter start to sprint away,
light spreading from her light step on damp sand.

## THERE'S NOTHING FINER THAN A BOY!

I look at myself looking at myself
from my mother's lap at three months.
What peculiar reversals, to see

myself so helpless I can't control
that ponderous head gravitating
so precariously on its neck-stem,

to see my sister and my mother laugh
at my helplessness, each wearing
a t-shirt printed with sea creatures

for my pleasure. It gives me the bends
just to look at it! I can't see much
from my mother's living lap except

the friendly blur that is my father
trying to take the definitive picture
of his family, to capture his daughter

and heir balanced two years apart
just like the Doctor wrote, to prove
his perfect timing before they grow up

and he can't remember their birthdays.
But it keeps going wrong, he keeps
slicing off feet and the tops of heads

with the dangerous edge of the frame,
he can't get it right! It's an arcade
of crazy mirrors, all these pictures

trying to warp me back into mother's hands,
the delicious pressure of her finger
on my sole, that cool palm on my neck . . .

It's my father's birthday. How could he
ask for anything better, don't we know
that we're his candles and cake and gifts,

what more could he want? *There's nothing
finer than a boy!* bragged the blue card
he taped in the album, and he believed it,

and so did my mother when she laughed
into the thoughtless face of her son
and thought she saw herself laughing back.

## VANISHING ACT

My mother disappeared into her children,
into her pictures of her children,
making only cameo appearances
for the last half of her life—
on holiday, at graduation, whenever
the composition demanded a mother-prop.

She abdicated the power of her image
willingly, there was no struggle,
when a camera appeared it triggered her reflex
to vanish behind it or out of frame,
she became more difficult
to photograph than a superstitious tribesman!

No more brilliant solos
at Daytona, in a mountain field, on a shiny coupé.
Every picture became a recital piece
for someone else, my mother bent
over the piano's arthritic keys, the invisible ground
from which other melodic lines could flower.

See how she hides behind her granddaughter
in this picture I took on top of Chimney Rock,
how she uses my father's arm
to erase as much of herself as possible?
She wishes the mist would lift from the valley lake
and take the rest of her.

But it doesn't. I wish I could say
as I stare at this late picture of my late mother
that I feel her hiding behind me again,
her knotted hands kneading my shoulders,
her sharp laugh parting my hair
as we stand on steep granite, our backs to the view.

# IV

# POCKET WATCH

    1.

We walked by the ghost of Wolfe's stone shop,
by the library with the wooden Indian
whose headdress I stroked on our weekly visits,
by the jaundiced adult book store

into Finkelstein's Pawn Shop on Pack Square,
its walls loud with stereos and guitars.
Mom and I stood at the splintered counter
and studied the trays of hocked pocket watches

and finally asked if we could see the Elgin.
"A good little watch," said the mustached man
as he unscrewed the back casing to show us
that perfect Swiss movement, those 17 jewels.

    2.

Even now, I get the same visionary thrill
I did that high-school graduation day

when I strapped on the loupe and saw
that precise paradise of underlying secrets,
wheels inside wheels, crisp gears and ratchets,
the pulsing mainspring like a blue-gray hair,
the blood-drop jewels winking at me . . .

It's like screwing the dome off a cathedral
and watching the doctrine of God unwind
in the palm of your hand.

3.

A few days ago, after her funeral, my father
showed me his father's pocket watch again,
a huge silver tumor
that must weigh several pounds.

"I want you to have this," he reminded me.
I nodded yes, but fingered
the slim doubloon killing time in my pocket.


4.

On the way home, I scrutinized
the inset circle of seconds eclipsing the 6,
the hour hand like a flattened spade,
the minute hand's skinny diamond,

the fine tread of the crown when pinched
between my index finger and thumb,
the almost classical frieze around its bezel.

And I pressed it to my ear and thought
of the mysteries wound inside,
how the ticking might simply stop at any time.

5.

The watch recites its stubborn trochees
to the birthmark hidden on my thigh.

Tonight I'll slip it from my pocket, a warm charm,
and bury it in a handkerchief on the dresser

to hush the leaky faucet of its seconds,
those steady increments of darkness

that would count me awake all night long,
the coiled heart that I have to wind tomorrow.

# WILDER BRAIN COLLECTION, CORNELL UNIVERSITY

    1.

Chalking the time for a test,
I squint through an odd seam of light
between the slates of blackboard:

a permanent display of brains
in the hall outside this classroom.

    2.

They float like pickled cauliflower
in a Scotch-rich brine,

shrunken buttocks
petrified in some remote scholarly bog.

    3.

"This collection began over a century ago
as a way for experimental psychologists to study
the relationship of the brain to the mind."

For years, they passed out tasteful bequest forms
at alumni dinners, just after dessert.

    4.

If you stare at the brains
like a kid trying to catch a minute hand moving,
eventually you'll see it:

they tremble.

Ever so slightly,
like exquisitely-tuned seismic instruments,
they tremble.

And some of them seem to be sweating.

   5.

There's Professor Wilder's brain,
a modest specimen, though one expert notes
"a wealth of convolutional development
in the parietal, occipital, and temporal regions."

And there are the rest of his colleagues,
a regular faculty meeting.

But the real celebrity is the murderer Ruloff,
his brain the second largest ever recorded,
so sickeningly big it barely fits
in the glass skull of his jar.

He too was a schoolteacher.
One day he killed his wife and child.
Later he escaped and wrote a "reputable" paper,
"Methods of the Formation of Language."

Someone finally tracked him down and hanged him
and cracked the huge nut of his head

and brought the meat here, a moral display.

    6.

Some of the brain lobes are chipped,
some cracked, their hemispherical symmetry
spoiled.

No surprises on the inside,
no mental geodes, just a smooth cross section
of proverbial gray matter.

And some of the brains are still trapped
in a stubborn membrane, a spidery web,
an almost invisible net.


    7.

That's exactly where my mother died,
in a cerebral hemorrhage
between the pia and the dura mater,
a stray vessel there sabotaging the brain.

*Did she feel a strange pressure beforehand?*
*Did she fall into light, or darkness, or nothing,*
*the cumulus of her neutral brain?*

    8.

It proved impossible to map
the intricate topography of the brain
and then use those contours to predict
or explain the patterns of a mind

so this collection was discontinued
years ago, the field discredited
as another radical branch of phrenology.
Most of the broken brains were thrown away.

    9.

I go back into the classroom,
watch the rows of heads inclined
in a kind of intellectual tropism,
as if their brains were drawn
to the light of the paper.

I think how recently my son
mastered the balance of his head,
how only last week my mother
bent to a bright page of words.

I write the final time on the board.

## SECRETS

    1.

My father and I prune the swayback branches
of the Christmas pine we planted in the yard
decades ago still glistening with tinsel,
its neat evergreen taper long since warped
into a shapeless shape. We trim branches
until they pile wreath-deep around the tree,
then dad suddenly says,
                            "Son, there's something
I feel like I ought to tell you but I can't."
"Sure you can, dad," I say, "you can tell me
anything"—expecting nothing. "Your mother,"
he begins, and I prepare to hear again
how long she'd wanted this tree cut back,
how many years she'd begged him to do the job.
"Your mother," he says, "she was an alcoholic."

    2.

On the night she died, a supernova
ignited the southern sky, the largest
since Kepler saw one with his naked eye
five years before Galileo's telescope.

That light had traveled a billion billion miles
from a star that exploded 170,000 years ago,
and it arrived the night my mother died.

3.

For a few sprung seconds, I feel suspended
above my body, like someone in shock
trying to stumble away from an accident.

But then things begin to focus, my hands
tacky with resin, my father cradling the saw,
saying she stopped drinking before I was born.

4.

At first, her drinking seems the missing clue,
the out-of-frame fact that casts its shadow
in all those pictures. It makes a kind of sense,
but it also interposes a curious filter
between me and every memory of my mother—
not a taint but a tint, the $n$th dimension
unimagined until now.
                    By *me*. Everybody else
already seems familiar with those lost years
and simply says, *I always thought you knew.*
And so an optimistic dread infects
the grief I've barely begun to admit:
what other secrets might yet come to light,
blistering toward us from the vacuum of the past?

5.

A star's life is a radiant balancing act
between its own fierce gravity and the energy
boiling outward from its core. When that tension

collapses, so does the star, which can start
another supernova like my late mother's,
a black hole from which nothing can escape.

6.

Can we really believe that one birth or death
and a dead star finally blazing forth
are somehow twinned, intentional, a sign

of favor, a celestial miracle
that we'll make holy with something as homely
as a star-topped tree twinkling with light?

7.

Such incredible connections!—
that the "calcium in our bones, the iron
in our hemoglobin, and the oxygen we all breathe
came from explosions like this one,"
that the shock wave of neutrinos
preceding the burst of that star's light
permeated everything on earth,
                              my mother
in a hopeless coma in a downtown hospital,
my father pacing the long lightless hours,
me frozen in a guilty sleep far north,
the tree whose only ornaments that night
were a gibbous moon, a skyful of dying stars,
and a cardinal's nest hidden on an upper branch.

## LAST BIRTHDAY

1.

The dogwood always brought its blossoms
tied in perfect pink gift-bows, but mother
hated her birthday anyway, that anniversary
of mere age. Every year, we tried again
to shock her into pleasure with our presents,
but there was a perpetual undertone of failure
in the rustle of tissue, in the grate of forks
cutting through a layer cake with no candles.

2.

Last year, I sat her at the kitchen table
with a cup of coffee, her eyes sworn closed,
then snapped Schubert's late C-major quintet
into her granddaughter's borrowed Walkman.

I whispered, "Happy birthday, mom," then clamped
the foam muffs over her ears and pressed PLAY.
A faint surf of sound drifted from her head,
which she began shaking, slowly. I reached
to turn the tape down or off, but she seized
my hand, still shaking her head, and began
to whisper, "Beautiful. Beautiful. Beautiful."

3.

Schubert bent to coffee and croissants
in a Vienna café, blinded by another headache.

He tried to erase it by loudly humming
his new Quintet, music he'd never hear performed.

He died two months later, not quite 32.
By then, those hummed notes were light-years away.

4.

I watch mother listen to the adagio,
its clear depths as much silence as sound,

a colloquy between sky and ground,
the inquisition of the violins

answered, anchored by the plucked heartstrings
of bass, our faithful mortal harp.

Gradually that sublime exchange
falters, stalls, comes to a near-halt . . .

Does every masterpiece, every piecemeal life
approach such collapse, its balance

fractured, on the verge of vanishing
like a star overwhelmed by its own forces?

       5.

Last week was her birthday, the first in years
she hadn't been forced to celebrate. But we
persisted: I wired a potted Easter lily

that dad dragged to the cemetery and posed
right over her heart, taking this snapshot
to send me as a kind of thank-you note.

It's terrifying, that plant—
so badly out of scale, taller than the dogwood
that casts its shallow shadow in the background,

forcing the soft door of her grave
with its rude health and heft and green,
its flowers blaring like apocalyptic sirens . . .

Soon they will bolt her birth date at her head,
the bright half of the couplet everybody writes.

       6.

*That passage,*
*melody swelling over pizzicato:*
*hear the strings weep for me,*
*the cellos moan, the violins keen?*

*Friends, don't fret,*
*I feel the music filling me*
*here in this house of bright wood,*
*death draws his long bow over,*
*I think my coffin may break into song!*

# · V ·

# GRACE

1.

Lois is grooming the five-gaited Morgan
named Salem. Soon her kid sister Molly
will come for the summer at Grace, this camp
in a fold of the Smokies near Tennessee,
owned by her father-in-law whose mission
is to convert the heathen wilderness
into board-feet, useful troops for the nation,
for the war so distant from this paradise
where timber is the only thing that ever dies.

Molly would rather comb this horse's coat
than her own red hair, a radiant thicket
surrounding a face so freckled she almost
seems more like a painting than flesh, a trick
of some Impressionist. She likes to flick
her fine mane, pretend to be "Philippa,
Pre-Raphaelite model, fourteenth mistress
of Rossetti!" *Too many books,* the elder
sister thinks, and invites Molly out for a summer

of instruction in the life of facts. And men.
Aside from her sequestered mother-in-law,
who stays in the stone bungalow with Glenn
Miller and a trunk of Luckies, bawling,
Lois is the only woman at all
among four dozen solid mountain men, who
saw and haul logs thicker than she is tall,
taller than the Flat Iron Building she knew
back in Asheville in business college, before her new

husband deported her to Grace, then shipped
out. She wants to show young Molly the real
image of men, as weary drones who tip
their caps when they pass, wolf every meal
in silence, smoke, sleep, and work. No ideals
needed out here: this is strictly duty,
she keeps the books and balances—feelings
have nothing to do with it. She hopes Molly
will heed her solid advice, rein in the folly

of a fourteen-year-old's faith in romance,
in Lancelots. *No heroes:* her husband
had written her this, from a trench, his pants
stiff with blood from supporting a dead friend,
a neighborhood boy Lois had known since
first grade. *There are no heroes . . .* Salem stares.
Lois gives him a final brush, then cleans
the combs. Mess bell will soon season the air
with dinner tones—and then her sister will be there.

    2.

Her father-in-law Harry had a manner
of grinning that gave away his practical
jokes before they had a chance. At dinner
that day, for example, Lois could tell
something was up, and, when the funny-smelling
meat was offered, she passed. "Come on honey,"
he pressed, "this is special stuff!" She lied. "Well,
Mr. Shuford, I snacked all morning, y'see.
I think I'll just have some bread and a cup of coffee."

Afterwards she snuck back to the kitchen
and asked the cook what it was. "Goat," he said,
"Old Bill"—the camp's late pet. "Was he tender?"
Before she could breathe, she saw the bright head
of Molly lighting the cracked window, and sped
outside. The sisters smothered each other
until Molly said, "Lois, I'm *star*-ved!
What's that good smell? Any left?" "Oh, brother,
you don't even want to know. —Tell me about mother."

They talked the day away, walking along
Cold Spring, taking an after-dinner ride
on Salem and his feisty cousin Winston
(named for Churchill, not the cigarette) toward
Max Patch, a bald, the perfect place to hide
because it was so open, with blue views
of three states from the summit. They defied
the common sense of sunset, and refused
to head back till they'd savored every ounce of news.

The trail had almost vanished when they heard
their note of hope: a bagpipe's drone and skirl.
"The Major!" they cried, and galloped ahead
toward the Salvation Army Mission Chapel
where Flora McIntosh played her farewell
to each day's light—tonight, "Jesus Shall Reign
Where'er the Sun." Her final tearful swell
had just faded when the girls rode up. "Saints
be praised!" she brayed, "a couple of careless pagans!"

The Major dispatched a message to Grace
that the sisters would be spending the night
with her at the Mission. She fixed a place
for them apart from the orphans, the sight
of whom caused Molly—their age—to weep. "Right!
Good to see you girls again! Settle back,
and let the Major tell you a tale that might
be hard to believe if it weren't for the fact
that *I was there!* I'd swear it on the biggest stack

of Bibles you could find—if I could swear,
which I can't. Well, it happened long ago
when I first brought the gospel way up here—
before they built the lumber mill, you know.
An old mountain man named Ledbetter was so
moonstruck when his ancient sister died
that he decided to *keep* her—said no
man would ever bury that body, defied
anyone to try, laid her in state on a side-

board and started a party. 'Weep at birth,
celebrate at death'—there's some merit to
that philosophy, especially if the earth
is as stingy as these hills. Well, he threw
a party that lasted for three days, you
could hear the music up at the Mission
from his holler down near Big Bend, it grew
louder and sloppier with every run
on his stash! On the night of the first day, someone

came and told me Miss Ledbetter was dead
but not quite gone. I saddled up my horse,
William Booth, said the Lord's Prayer, and headed
out, down that moonshine trail to hell. Of course
everyone was holy drunk—no remorse
yet. Music everywhere: banjos, fiddles,
guitars, jew's harps, jugs, wash-tub bass. I forced
my way to the kitchen: in the middle
sat Mr. L., his sister to the side, a little

ripe already. I shook his hard hand. 'Sir,
my sympathies on your loss.' He sat stiff
as *her*. 'Let me help you give a proper
burial, before the odor gets bad, if
you—' His shotgun clicked once; the old man sniffed.
'Don't smell nothing, myself. Good evening, ma'am.'
I tugged at my Salvation neckerchief,
said a quick prayer for guidance and a *damn,*
and left. But on my way out I pulled aside Ham

Brookshire and asked him to come see me soon
as he could. By the time he snuck away
I had an idea: 'How's the white lightning
holding out, Ham?' 'A little low.' 'OK.
Get all the strong whiskey you can. I'll pay.
Take it back to Ledbetter's and get them
so drunk they all fall asleep. Don't say
anything suspicious. Tomorrow I'll come
when it's quiet, and we'll steal her away. Hunt up Shem

(Ham's brother) to help us.' It was early
on the second day. Shem came, and I set
him to digging a grave (on our property—
it's right outside, girls). There was noise yet
from Big Bend, all day long, and so I let
Shem try his hand at a coffin: crooked,
rough, but good enough for the job. He met
me back at the Mission at dawn: we looked
like a couple of bandits, with bandanas hooked

over our noses—to keep out the smell.
How we managed to sneak down that bad road
and across the yard to the window—well,
Lord knows why those sleeping drunks just laid
and let Ham slide Miss L. into the bed
of our wagon, and let us creak on off
with our spoils. Maybe the Lord himself hid
us in a kind of mist, like when Christ left
the temple under threat of death. Anyway, our theft

was a success: we buried that woman fast,
believe you me. Later that day, here came
Mr. Ledbetter himself, with a vast
hangover and his shotgun, almost lame
from the wake. I was so scared (it's no shame
to say it) I had to sit down at my desk
before I could call, 'Come in.' 'Some folks claim
you took my sister.' I nodded once. Dusk
snuck in at his heels, his head was a large dark disk

whose features I couldn't read. I waited
to die. Then that shadow of a man bent
slightly, and spoke. 'I'm sorry. I appreciate
your trouble, Miss McIntosh.' As he went,
my voice unfroze. 'I know your sister meant
the world to you, Mr. Ledbetter. She's
under the willow oak.' Whatever I spent
to get her there was all worth it, to see
that old man rise from that new grave, mud on his knees.

What kept him from killing me? What strange grace
made me act, made him repent? The good Lord
works in mysterious ways and places,
sisters, even here. Why, my bagpipe chords
brought you safely here tonight, right? —No more:
it's time you two girls rested. Say your prayers,
don't forget." Major Flora filled the door
with her own solid shadow; on the stairs
of sleep, the sisters heard her humming bless the air.


    3.

Lois and Molly wake the next morning,
a cool June day in 1945,
with different morals from the same story:
Molly, that it's great to be alive
in a world where men are so protective
of their loved ones; Lois, that men are fools,
drunken, violent, shameful, possessive
idiots. Each sister, fond but willful,
hopes the other learns her lesson, and is grateful.

Their days have a hazy rhythm, like the hills
surrounding Grace Lumber Mill. Lois rises
at dawn, a married woman now, who fills
her hours with other peoples' work. She prizes
that time in the steamy stable, the eyes
of Salem wanting oats, the lull before
each day's storm. On her way to the office,
she stops by the commissary for one more
coffee, brewed from a busted still. Then it's off to war.

Molly, a dozen years younger, a girl
on summer vacation, never leaves bed
till lunch—sleeping in, then reading her world
into being. Lois says, "Go ahead,
but be careful," when Molly sticks her hot head
into the office and asks, "Can I borrow
Salem for a while?" She rides that purebred
stallion all afternoon, far as Sorrow
Gap sometimes, and always promises, "Tomorrow

I won't go so far, sister." But she does.
Evenings, they walk or ride along the spring,
exhausted, their conversation abuzz
with family, the day, imaginings
of the distant future—sisters moving
in the vicinity of grace for just one
summer. Sometimes the Major comes, singing
hymns to unsaved nature, her Salvation
bonnet brimming with tales for their edification.

4.

One day Molly missed dinner, and later burst
into her sister's cabin. "Lois, wait
till you hear about this! Salem got thirsty
near Max Patch, so I hitched him to the gate
by the pool, and walked toward the crest. Well, straight
ahead, on the Altar Rock, sat this guy
writing on a notepad. I couldn't wait
for him to turn around, so I said, 'Hi!
What're you writing?' He jumped, then smiled, and said, 'I—

I'm a poet.' He handed me a page:
it wasn't bad! We got to talking. Walt
was his name—like Whitman, you know? His age?
Oh, 20, 25, not much. He told
me he was from San Francisco, which he called
'Parnassus of the West.' When I asked him
what he was doing *here,* he kind of stalled,
but finally said, 'I work these days with them,'
pointing to a group of men just below the rim

of trees. 'And who are *they?*' 'Forest Service
volunteers,' he said. 'We help put out fires
and help prevent them before they start.' This
puzzled me: '*Volunteers?* Why?' He perspired
so bad it dripped on his poem. 'I'm a liar,'
he said, 'or at least I'm not telling the whole
truth. We all are conscientious objectors,
CO's. We refused to go to war. Our goal
is peace, like the government's, but we keep our souls

apart from violence. This is what we do
instead of fighting.' I stepped away. 'Please
don't be afraid. We'll be here for a few
weeks. Come see me again.' Lois, my knees
felt like water, They still do." A dark breeze
swept through the cabin: rain soon. Molly shut
the door, and sat. "Oh, what should I do? He's—"
"I'll tell you what he is," said Lois: "nuts,
or else he'd be in uniform. No ifs, ands, or buts."

But Molly went back to see him, and became
a kind of disciple of Saint Walter,
as Lois referred to him, her old claim
on Molly waning. Once the quiet sisters
rode together to Max Patch; on the Altar
Rock he sat, crosslegged, with thick black glasses,
a homely man in moccasins. Lingering,
Lois watched one "conversation" on the grass
where Walt and the infatuated Molly held class—

or rather, he lectured, she listened. "Once
people would have homesteaded that valley,"
he said, "had farms and children, a license
to live. Now they forsake their family
and go abroad, and murder, and probably
never come back . . ." Lois rode off. Like most
prophets, he was too nearsighted to see
his effect on the lonely local host
of the faithful, how they crave him and not the ghost

of his God. And anyway, how could she
stand there and listen, with a husband gone
for over three years, doing his duty
by God and Uncle Sam and her, the icon
of his single snapshot fading in the sun
on her dusty bureau? She'd only heard
from him two times a year, though he'd begun
(so he wrote) "a letter every day. My word
of honor, hon. You know you're my only lovebird."

5.

Grace was a noisy chaos, with the mill
turning the National Forest into logs
like so many matchsticks, seen from the hills
above, some floating in the sweet ripe bogs
of sawdust and water in which the dogs
would swim, pulpy mutts. Huge trucks and tractors,
bulldozers for cutting roads, a dense fog
of equipment—each piece a character.
And Lois herself was acknowledged director

of operations, since her in-law Harry
fancied himself a backwoods Vanderbilt,
not a mere lumber businessman. Sherry
was his drink, every evening. Out of guilt
he gave the men a chapel, with a fine gilt
pulpit, where Major Flora McIntosh
preached Salvation twice a week. And he built
his wife a garden gazebo, a posh
unused retreat, overlooking the summer squash.

He loved to give Lois pets, the stranger
the better. Once he brought a flying squirrel
to camp in a gunny sack; a ranger
had caught him. "Guess what I got in here, girl,"
he said, grinning—and it burst like shrapnel
around the office for the next three days,
then sailed out the window. There was an owl
Harry kept in a cage, whose yellow gaze
could freeze Lois's sweat, leave her useless and dazed—

his master, the son of a worker, killed
in action. But worst of all were the snakes,
big rattlers that the timber men uphill
brought in for bounty, a buck apiece. "Steak
and skin, that's what my pal in Florida, Jake,
wants 'em for." Lois felt rattlers at her feet
in the office, they poisoned the dark lake
of her dreams, she was even afraid to eat
for fear Harry would serve them. (He did, as "gator meat.")

But Lois survived his mad menagerie.
She kept the camp on track, dressing the part:
work shirt and pants and boots, no flattery
necessary. Since Molly lost her heart
to Walt on Max Patch, Lois worked harder
than ever: her evenings were long dim hours
of ledgers, orders, typewriter, time card,
with too much time to think about a rumor
that the Pacific war might end before the summer.

6.

One long twilight Molly materialized
at the office screen. "Lois, can we talk
for a while?" It seems Walt too had realized
that something might be in the air. "We walked
the Trail toward Snowbird today. Walt said, 'Look.'
I laughed—he was pointing into Tennessee
like some frontier explorer—but he shook
his head. 'No. Over there, past Knoxville. We
can't quite see it, but there's a new laboratory

whose power can alter the world forever.'
He talked about Oak Ridge, a secret project,
a bomb made of atoms. 'We must *never*
use it!' he hissed. 'Why not,' I objected,
'if it ends the war?' 'Only in one respect,'
he said: 'this fighting might be stopped for now,
but soon a worse war will start, that will infect
the tissue of our everyday lives. How
will it all end? Can we beat this sword into a plow?

I don't know.' He paused. 'But I think they'll ship
us back west soon. I'm not sure when; I'll try
to let you know.' " Molly stopped; her top lip
sealed her mouth as she struggled not to cry.
The sun set like a bomb on that July.
The sisters sat in a brilliant shadow,
their days of Grace numbered, their sanctuary
endangered—one worried that love might go,
the other that, after blank years, love might come home.

A few days later Lois skipped camp lunch
(Harry was grinning) and went out to the barn.
Salem was feeding; she could hear the crunch
of his big teeth. Molly had slung her arm
around his bent neck: with the open palm
of her other hand, she'd give him some oats,
then take a bite herself. In some alarm,
Lois cried, "Molly!" "They stick in your throat,"
she said, "but they taste OK. And they make Salem's coat

*so* shiny!" They laughed and hugged each other
for a long time. "I talked to Walt today,"
Molly breathed. "He said there was another
woman in his life—his wife. And that they,
the CO's, were going now." Salem neighed
as Lois hid the embers of Molly's head
deep in her jacket, unable to say
a word for the sudden suffocating dread
that Corporal Gene Shuford was missing or dead.

Late the very next day, somebody knocked
on the open office door, a courtesy
unheard-of there in Grace. Lois rocked back
and called, "Yes?", and nearly fell when Percy
Early, the ancient mailman, croaked, "Missy?
Special Delivery. Overseas. For you."
She locked the door on his "Lord have mercy"
and sat down on the desk, alone. *For you,*
she thought. She noticed the stationery was blue.

"Dear Lois, don't worry, I'm fine, no scars.
I don't think they'll be chiseling my name
on a veteran's memorial. I'm no martyr.—
I'll be brief here. I won't be coming home
anytime soon; I've signed up for more time
in Europe, to help out. I'm not the man
I was; the drinking's much worse; I can't seem
to stop. I think we should divorce. What's mine
is yours, everything. Take it. I'm sorry. Love, Gene."

Lois studied the letter for a while.
It seemed to be authentic. And although
Gene could have settled matters with more style
or gotten killed and left a little dough,
Lois wasn't surprised, or mad, or low.
She felt . . . *relieved*. It was over and done,
she could finish the summer here and go
back to town. "But I won't tell anyone,"
she said through the window to the pacific sun.

    7.

A week or two later, Molly rides back
to Max Patch. She stops by the office first
to ask permission, to pick up a snack,
to see if Lois can come. Her sister
is on the porch, tacking up a poster:
NEW LUMBER FOR SHIPS! "Oh, Molly, I'd love
to—but I can't, I have to meet with Mr.
Shuford soon. Here, take the dogs, and my lunch.
Stay all day if you want to. Be careful! Good luck."

Molly sets out on Salem, the Shepherds
in their wake—past the millworkers' cabins,
the chapel, the thick Victory garden. Birds
attend them, wildflowers flicker gently in
the pasture, the day is a private wedding,
Molly the bride. Ahead of her, the road
reluctantly snakes out of sight, heading
for the summit, littered with rich shadows,
a pungent tunnel of evergreens and leaf-mold.

Max Patch is a four-mile ride. By the time
they arrive, its spring-pool is a miracle,
a draft of heaven on the tongue. Their climb
across the bald is mild, a soft ramble
through buttercups and uncut grass. Several
false summits swell; Molly and Salem know
not to pause, to press on to that table
of slate, the Altar Rock, where the view flows
unhindered in every direction, in blue rows

of mountains and valleys that never stop,
everything slowly refined into sky
at the horizon, as if God had dropped
that Rock during creation at the eye
of this Appalachian puddle, then fired
it fast, fixing these geologic waves
for Molly to sit at their focus. Why
*was* Max Patch bald, were there *really* huge caves
inside, was this a ritual rock where Cherokee braves

sacrificed virgins? Molly could rehearse
all the legends, and often did, looking
for Indian hieroglyphics, a deep curse
or blessing carved into the Altar Rock,
a verbal arrowhead, a clue, a shock
from the inscrutable past. But not today.
She lets the animals loose, a winded flock,
then sits crosslegged at the heart of the great
warm stone, facing west, to eat lunch and meditate.

She thinks about the War, a feature movie
shot far from this peaceful border. No one
seems to suffer here, really, not even
those who lose boys. *Did it matter who won
such a war?* Walt had asked. "We can't just run
from it," Lois said, "and nothing can keep
war out of our hearts." The same dog-day sun
ripens crops and rots corpses, shines on sheep
and bombs. Molly thinks of Walt, gone. She falls asleep.

——She wakes in a panic: what day is it?
Where's Salem? the Shepherds? What *was* that dream?
Her skin is embossed by the rock's blanket.
She remembers a plane, a flash, a scream—
nothing more. Silence. "I've got to get home,"
Molly thinks, mounting Salem, with a shrill
whistle for the sleeping dogs. Down the dome
of grass they race, Molly stopping to fill
her eyes one last time with the perfect prospect, till

the dogs bark her back to the path, begging
for water already. No time for that,
for trailside digressions: she keeps egging
the Shepherds downward, she constantly pats
Salem's slick neck, they are all on a hunt
for some sly quarry, her fox-colored hair
bounding. At the Mission, for a moment,
they pause: a kind of music haunts the air,
rising from the valley like hickory smoke. "Why, they're

ringing the chapel bell! Let's go!" And so
they fly the final mile to camp, afraid
of another disaster, a ton of new-
cut logs on a man, a runaway blade,
Lois dead somehow . . . By the time they make
the outskirts of Grace, its single dirt street
is packed with people, laughing, crying. "Take
this," Molly says to the first man she meets,
handing Salem's bridle. "What happened?" "Oh my, sweet

Jesus, ain't you heard? It's ended! The war
is over!" Molly sprints till she's dizzy,
shouting for Lois—who waves from the door
of the chapel. "It's all over, Molly!"
*Over forever, for everybody,*
she thinks. "Come over here and ring the bell!"
The sisters fuse hands. Inside the belfry,
the Major is waiting: "Come on now, girl!"
Molly steps, and seizes the knotted rope, and falls.

A NOTE ON THE AUTHOR

MICHAEL McFEE was born in Asheville and lives in Durham, North Carolina. He has been visiting poet at Cornell, Lawrence, and the University of North Carolina at Chapel Hill. His poems have appeared in *Poetry, Hudson Review, Virginia Quarterly Review,* and *The Nation,* among other places. His previous books of poems are *Vanishing Acts* (Gnomon, 1989) and *Plain Air* (Florida, 1983). He has also collaborated with photographer Elizabeth Matheson in *To See* (North Carolina Wesleyan College Press, 1991).

A NOTE ON THE BOOK

*Sad Girl Sitting on a Running Board* was composed in Bembo with Eric Gill's Perpetua used for display. Composition by Graphic Composition, Inc. It was printed on acid-free paper by Thomson-Shore, Inc. in an edition of 1,200 copies.